10 Leadership Insights

Every Leader Needed... Yesterday!

10 LEADERSHIP
INSIGHTS

Every Leader Needed... Yesterday!

Aaron Daniel Chavez, M.Ed.

The Author

Aaron Chavez is known for being a turnaround educational leader after successfully leading some of the most challenging school districts in the state of Washington. He was also honored in 2002 in the prestigious *Who's Who of America's Teachers*. He is the President and Founder of the United States- based Gladiator Leadership & Coaching. He can be contacted for speaking, training, and executive coaching through his website Gladiatorcoach.com or email: gladiatorcoach@icloud.com.

Acknowledgements

I would like to first thank my mother Elaine Chavez and my father Dan Chavez for their support and love. They both taught me the value of hard work and that my dreams were always possible. I would also like to thank my sister Tawnee and my brother Shawn Chavez for his inspiration. He has shown the entire family and world that it is never too late for a comeback. Of course, I have to thank my grandparents Mel & Leona Dickinson. They invested in me early on and I hope one day to be able to fill their shoes. I would also like to thank my children, Tehya Leona Chavez, Bing Alan Mel Chavez, and Inara Hazel Chavez, as well as Chanan, my fiancée, for their prayers, love and support. I hope that this book adds value to others in some small way and shows that being your imperfect self is perfection.

Yet he did not waver through unbelief regarding the promise of God, but was strengthened in his faith and gave glory to God.

—Romans 4:20

The true gift of life is the sure knowledge of death. For without it, Man would not strive to leave their mark on the world

—Unknown

Contents

Introduction

I REMEMBER VIVIDLY MY dad, Dan Chavez, telling my little brother Shawn and me when we were kids that he was raising us to be leaders, not followers. He would sit us both down and make us write out our goals, making sure that we included where we wanted to be in five years. As you know, when you're 12 years old, that's the last thing you want to be doing. Riding our bikes, catching bugs, or playing with our cousins was much, much higher on the list, however we did it reluctantly for Dad.

I remember that at the top of my list for a long time was wanting to be a police officer. In fact, I remember telling friends on the playground that my dad was a police officer. Our dad was actually a cement mason, just like his dad Louis Hilbert Chavez. My grandpa, "Bunny" we called him, spent a lifetime finishing concrete, after serving and being wounded on the island of Leyte during World War II. Grandpa Bunny, like my dad, would rise up through the leadership construction ranks to foreman, general foreman, and then superintendent level positions.

Later in my childhood, my dad's leadership ability was noticed by a company named Rust Engineering who built paper mills around the United States. After that, my family and I began moving almost yearly. I spent 4th through 12th grades moving from Washington state to Tennessee, then to Minnesota, then to Maine and finally back to Washington as my dad helped build these paper mills. It wasn't fun leaving friends at the end of each school year and I remember not being really too happy (putting it nicely) with my dad for making us move so much. However, of course, in reflection now, the things I learned while moving helped me further down the road as I worked construction and moved up from teacher to principal and finally to a school superintendent.

In seventh grade in Washougal, Washington, while my dad worked at the nearby paper mill in Camas, Washington (supervising his brother and Dad Bunny for a time), I would have some teachers come into my life who would plant the seeds of becoming a teacher. I had a lot of great public school teachers, but the ones I remember the most were Mr. Bright, Mr. Burnham, and Mr. Cass. They were teachers and coaches of mine who would inspire me to eventually graduate from Eastern Washington University with a Bachelor's degree in Social Sciences.

After graduating from college, I promptly moved back to Washougal and began substitute teaching in the surrounding school districts. The highlight was being called in to "sub" for Mr. Bright and Mr. Burnham's classes. However, after I had a student literally empty everything off a teacher's desk and throw it in the air, I learned quickly that substitute teaching wasn't all it was cracked up to be. I was fortunate that after that first school year subbing, I landed a teaching job in the Finley School District, where my dad and other family graduated. When they handed me the keys to my first classroom, my hands were shaking a bit because of the pressure I felt walking under my dad's and other family members' senior pictures on the wall.

I spent six years in the district, and I had some great years teaching at both the high school and junior high levels. In my last few years in Finley, a few colleagues would plant the seed that I needed to get my principal credentials, to which I would promptly reply that I didn't like red tape or politics and would never become a principal. Little did I know, about two years later I would do just that in a small community named Almira. I served as their principal for one year, and then in my second year would take on both the principal and superintendent roles. My growing family of three kids, Tehya, Bing, and Inara, lived in Almira for four years before I became the school superintendent in Brewster, Washington. About a year before getting the Brewster gig, I read in the "Spokesman Review" about a discrimination lawsuit that Brewster was going through. Of course, I remember saying that I would never work in a district dealing with those kinds of issues. However, a year later, you know what happened!

Both Almira and Brewster were great communities with each of them having their own special leadership challenges for me as a superintendent. In 2008, just as I settled into my first year as the Brewster superintendent, the "Great Recession" hit.

During my first spring break, my business manager informed me that because of the state's budget issues, we were expecting at least a million-dollar budget deficit. Needless to say, we survived. However, I found out quickly that by cutting a budget in a district with a history of levy failures, where teachers had volunteered in the past to coach for free, they were not keen to hear that there were more budget issues on the way.

Three years later, I became the superintendent of the Wahluke School District in Mattawa, Washington. When I took the reins July 1st, 2010, the district was on the state's lowest 50 list. My team and I worked quickly, and after a tumultuous March, 2011 board meeting, we restructured four of the six schools. Seven years later, we would also be a one-to-one district with every student, preschool through twelfth grade, having an iPad. Teachers also had MacBooks, projectors and Apple TVs. I'm very proud of the work we did in Wahluke, Brewster and Almira.

I've learned a lot as a leader over that time. And, of course, I made some mistakes along the way. However, now in reflection, I want to share some leadership insights so that up and coming leaders whose parents are having them write out goals, or someone who is just starting their career, can learn from some of my experiences when their time comes to lead.

Mark Zuckerberg, CEO of Facebook.com

INSIGHT #1
Influence

"Leadership is influence, nothing more, nothing less.

—John Maxwell

A s a leader, you have tremendous influence. Being ultimately responsible for your business's results and overall culture is just the tip of the iceberg when it comes to what a leader has influence over.

I learned over time when I became a formal leader that people would come calling early to begin influencing my thinking on priorities and people I had working for me. Sometimes these people's perceptions and thinking would be 100% accurate, other times just wrong. Most times, though, it was somewhere in the middle.

When I think of this insight, a good example is Tolkien's *Lord of the Rings: The Two Towers* movie. It was one of my favorites of the Lord of the Rings movies because of the character Gríma, called Wormtongue. He is introduced in *The Two Towers* as the chief advisor to King Théoden of Rohan and henchman of Saruman. Gríma's character in the movie serves as the flatterer, liar, and manipulator of King Théoden. If you watched the movie, you remember the king seemed to be in a trance because of Wormtongue's influence over him. It wasn't until Gandalf breaks the spell that the king can see things as they truly are.

As a leader, I seem to dissect everything through a leadership lens, and while watching the character Wormtongue manipulate King Théoden, I wondered to myself, who is my Wormtongue? Who is trying to influence me? That is an important insight that I believe every leader needs to be aware of.

Since we're using Lord of the Rings characters to emphasize this insight, another important question is, who is your Gandalf? Who's the person(s) that can give you a clear, accurate and unbiased picture of the reality you're facing as a leader? Now, don't go thinking everyone around you might be a Wormtongue. The point is to have an awareness that because of your influence as a leader, you will have people who will try to influence your thinking. One of the most important things you can do is gather data and make your own decisions on the people and situations you will encounter as a leader.

John Maxwell's Law of the Inner Circle also illustrates this insight. The law states that a leader's potential comes from those closest to him - the team. Who is currently on your team that is helping you reach your potential as a leader? Who's on your team weakening you as a leader? I know it's painful to even think about, but many times one team member can dramatically weaken a whole team.

Another real-life example of how weak team members can hurt or help a leader, as well the entire team, is some of President Donald Trump's cabinet picks. Some believe President Trump selected a risky (weak) team member in General Flynn shortly after he won the election. Flynn was selected as his national security advisor and eventually pled guilty to lying to the FBI after he misled officials about his contact and work with the Russians. On the other hand General Mattis the secretary of defense is believed to be one of his strongest team members.

As a leader, making sure your inner circle is strong and having an awareness that people will try and influence you is important. It's very important to make sure their influence on you is healthy and strengthens your leadership potential.

Some questions to consider...

- Who is your Wormtongue? Exaggerator? Gossip? Sky is always rising or falling person?

- Who is your Gandalf(s)? Who do you trust for an honest, unbiased perspective?

- What's at stake if you're influenced by the wrong person(s)?

- Who's in your inner circle?

George W. Bush 43 president of the United States.

INSIGHT # 2
Documentation

> Your memory is the glue that binds your life together; everything you are today is because of your amazing memory. You are a data collecting being, and your memory is where your life is lived.
>
> —Kevin Horsley

I F YOU'RE ANYTHING like me when I first began taking on leadership roles, I seemed to have a great memory for people, places and times. Of course, I was much younger and kept limited notes except for when dealing with personnel issues. However, now after reflecting on 20+ years of experience, I cannot stress enough how important it is to document conversations and incidents or situations you find yourself in as a leader.

Years ago, I remember meeting with a customer (parent) regarding their son. I worked hard at knowing my students' names and trying to connect in some way with them. This student and I would occasionally talk in the hallway during transitions between classes and I, for some reason, began making the gesture that I had my eyes on him by pointing to my eyes and then pointing at him with those two fingers. It was an innocent gesture done with a smile and I meant nothing from it. However, the mother of this child for some crazy reason thought that I was picking on her son. She scheduled a meeting with me and, to my surprise, brought up the gesture and proceeded to accuse me of bullying her son. I almost thought she was joking until her face turned red and I saw the vein sticking out on her forehead. I promptly apologized for any perception that I would ever bully a student. I've found apologizing even when you're probably right is the best course of action. Also remember a parent always has the right to advocate for their children.

As a leader you should also be aware of something called the *3% rule*, but on days there is a full moon it can feel more like 5% to 7%. You're probably asking what is the 3% rule? Well, I'm not sure how accurate it truly is, but it deals with people who have significant mental health issues. Actually, Newsweek reported in 2014 that 18% or 1 in 5 Americans suffer from a mental health issue. So, if you're running a business, coffee shop, restaurant, construction site, etc., occasionally one of the *3%* will come into your place of business and you need to have a protocol for staff on how to interact them in a professional and in a caring way. Training yourself and your staff to de-escalate people and situations is always important.

The movie *Horrible Bosses*, even though it's a comedy, illustrates this perfectly. If you have a boss who is a 3 percenter document, document, document.

The best ways I've found are the following:

- Keep a daily or weekly journal (written or digital) that includes dates, times and what exactly happened during your work week. It's important to say exactly how you felt and tell the story of exactly what occurred.

- Email yourself a quick memo if an incident occurs. Also, include date, time, and exactly what was said much like a police officer would write a report.

- Also, don't be afraid to have your secretary or another colleague sit in as a witness.

Some questions to consider...

- How are you currently documenting conversations? Situations? Incidents?

- Who do you call to coach you when you need help working with a difficult staff member, customer?

- How are you going to document in the future?

- Who can you use for a witness?

- Who is on your 3% list? Customers? Staff?

- What is your plan or protocol for you and your staff to deal with a 3 percenter?

Who's in your "Bad Apple" picture frame?

INSIGHT #3
Bad Apples

> A bad attitude can literally block love,
> blessings, and destiny from finding you.
> Don't be the reason you don't succeed.
>
> —Unknown

ATTITUDE IS EVERYTHING. Ask any coach, teacher, or leader if they want a person with a bad attitude on their team. They'll say no way! Or more than likely "Hell No!" Why? Well, because a person with a bad or toxic attitude will ruin your team faster than you can say, "Lickety split."

I learned early in my career as an athletic coach, teacher, and then later when I began running school districts, that bad apples affect performance. Not only my performance, but potentially anyone's who they come into contact with. The best way to describe it is like a flu virus. First, a few people catch it and then it spreads down a whole hallway. With email, text, and

Skype/FaceTime nowadays, it can spread even quicker through a business or community.

A good example happened early in my teaching career. I taught in the infamous portables where mice would crawl up on my desk at night and leave me surprises. I taught across the hall from a veteran teacher who had the worst attitude you could imagine. Between classes we would talk in the hallway and he would complain about the principal, schedule, students, weather, workload, pop machine, his girlfriend, his dog, the Seahawks, etc. Before long, I was complaining too and began expressing my complaints to someone further down the hall. It didn't change until his classroom moved to another part of the school.

Another example of this is the recent Trump verses Clinton presidential election and Russia's purchase of ads to help swing votes. Now, I'm not saying bad apples purchase ads on Facebook, but words, whether in email, video, meme, or verbal form affect a person's brain chemistry. Words that stress people out release cortisol, a stress hormone, into the brain. That chemical stays in the brain for over 24 hours and screws people's thinking and decision-making up.

If you're running a business and you have a bad apple staff member sending "flamers" out via email or in text form, you have some work to do as a leader. Calling a spade a spade and documenting bad apple behavior is some of the most difficult and most critical work you do as a leader.

Some recent research on bad apples and team effectiveness by Will Felps, Terence R. Mitchell and Eliza Byington will shock you like it did me. They examined the impact of three different types of bad apples. They were team members who were deadbeats (withholders of effort); downers (who express pessimism, anxiety, insecurity and irritation); and jerks (who violate interpersonal norms of respect). The experiment found that having just one bad apple can bring down performance by 30% to 40%.

Now, as a business leader, you're probably asking what a 30% to 40% decline in performance equates to in lost revenue? Test scores? Absenteeism? Customer service? Job satisfaction? Turnover? Employee engagement? I don't know, but I do know that I personally don't go back to a store where I had poor customer service. And I know a lot of people don't. In most cases, they go home and at a minimum, tell their partner, and maximum, they share with everyone how they were treated online.

I believe that bad apples end careers, close businesses and ultimately are the cause of many issues businesses face. I remember years ago I had a bad apple who looked like my grandpa Mel Dickinson. Rather than document this person's issues appropriately, we kept discipline mostly at the verbal level and in his year-end evaluations. To be honest, I kinda of liked the guy when he wasn't making my life miserable with his inappropriate, and at times, unsafe behavior. Ultimately, we ended up terminating him after an incident and, of course, he grieved through his union. He never came back, but it ended up costing us lawyer fees and a small settlement because his behavior was not documented thoroughly.

Some questions to consider...

- Who are the bad apples in your business?

- How have you documented their bad apple behavior?

- Who is currently being influenced by a bad apple in your organization?

- What kind of training has your staff received on how to document and evaluate bad apples?

- What is at stake if you do nothing with your bad apples?

Marissa Mayer, ex-CEO of YAHOO

INSIGHT # 4

Eight Hazardous Leadership Behaviors

> A man should never be ashamed he has been in the wrong, which is but saying that he is wiser today than he was yesterday.
>
> —Alexander Pope

C OMING UP THROUGH the ranks as a leader takes time, and on the way up most of us make lots and lots of mistakes. As a superintendent, principal, teacher, and parent, I've made a lot of them. However, here are a few we need to monitor closely in our team members and in ourselves. Past U.S. presidents and world leaders have commented about the intoxication of influence, power and leadership. All we have to do is watch the nightly news and see examples of these eight hazardous leadership behaviors. World leaders, famous actors, and even you and I can show these behaviors if we don't monitor our intentions and hearts as leaders closely.

Here are eight leadership behaviors in no particular order:

1. **Over-analyzation**: This leader requires too much data before they can act. Team members see these leaders as not able to make decisions in a decisive manner. This behavior can lead to some very bad consequences for a leader. One of them is that staff will gossip about your inability to act and may eventually go to someone else who is able to make the big decisions. Your credibility will also suffer. If you find yourself occasionally having this behavior, make sure to make decisions during emergencies thoughtfully and quickly. But with decisions where you have more time, simply let staff know that you're a leader who makes "data based decisions," and that you will review the data with your team and make a decision as soon as possible.

2. **Impulsivity**: This leader makes decisions too quickly before thinking through all the variables. This trait is just the opposite of over-analyzation. Like all these traits, sometimes they're hard wired into your DNA and you have to make an effort to be very conscious and aware. An executive coach can help a leader with this behavior by working with them on when this behavior manifests itself. Developing new habits and slowing down and gathering more data is the key to helping this hazardous behavior.

3. **Invulnerability**: This leader believes it won't happen to them and that things will always go their way. This

behavior comes to the surface often when a leader has accomplished some significant milestone or had a recent success. I cannot stress enough that if you have the feeling of "invulnerability," as a leader you need to re-evaluate your thinking. Leaders must know that they are very vulnerable because they are often in a very public position and their words and actions can and will be "sliced and diced." The pendulum as a leader is always swinging. One day you're the hero and the next minute you're the goat! Governor Chris Christie is an excellent example of the hero to goat leadership pendulum swings. From 2009 to 2013, he was considered a hero in the Republican Party. He was even being considered by many to run for president in 2012. Time Magazine even had him on the cover with title "The Boss." Little did he know that during the next four years he would swing from being the hero to the goat nation-wide. The infamous bridge scandal and numerous investigations soured people's taste of the once popular leader.

4. **EGO - Arrogance**: This leader believes that they can do and say anything they want without consequences. They may also deep down believe they're better than others. They may feel they're smarter, more articulate, more skilled, better trained... the list can go on and on. Younger leaders can have this trait early in their career. If not addressed and coached early, these leaders may burn bridges with more veteran leaders because they do not value and/or are not aware of the experience, knowledge and battles that have been fought during these veteran leaders' career spans.

5. **Resignation:** The leader believes and articulates out loud and frequently to staff that the odds are stacked against them. This behavior gives staff a sense of hopelessness and can create low-moral and low staff engagement, just to name a few. This trait may be found in more veteran leaders who have been in unhealthy systems or organizations. Language use is usually the first indicator of this trait. You may hear or say: *we can't, the odds are stacked against us, that will never work here...* etc. If you're a leader who uses this kind of language, you will lose credibility as a leader and your staff may not buy into what you have to offer.

6. **Fear:** The leader is afraid to have real conversations, make staffing moves, etc., for fear of the consequences from a group or individual. We are all human and fear and doubt can manifest itself in all of us. New leaders may sometimes be afraid of making that first big decision, and leaders in unhealthy systems or organizations may have this trait as a result of where they are in their career or current position.

7. **Lack of Awareness:** This leader does not have awareness of: systems, connections, influence, thinking gets stuck, power of relationships, blind spots (listening, micro-managing), language, does not honor previous work & experience, humor, talks more than listens, body language, interrupting, etc.) roles, differing perspectives, etc.

8. **Communication Errors/Ethical Issues:** This leader may share sensitive, confidential information to staff on lower

levels of the organizational chart, creating uncertainty, fear, rumors, gossip, etc.

9. The leader may also over communicate or under communicate. They may also give the impression of a lack of transparency. The leader chooses language (words) that escalate situations, staff, etc. The leader's vision and messaging may be inconsistent and cannot be communicated effectively from leader to leader.

Some questions to consider...

- Which of these leadership behaviors am I most susceptible to?

- Which of the behaviors have I shown recently?

- Who do I know that would give me honest feedback if I'm showing these behaviors?

- What's at stake if I begin showing any of these behaviors?

Elon Musk, CEO of Tesla.

INSIGHT # 5

Relationships

"People don't care how much you know until they know how much you care"

—John Maxwell

When I was first hired as the principal of a kindergarten through eighth grade school in Almira, Washington, I was on a mission. The mission was to improve the school by any means necessary and building relationships wasn't at the top of my to-do list. In fact, I remember telling a staff member something to the effect I wasn't there to make friends, I was there to move the school forward. I was so wrong and so green, looking back now.

Fortunately for me, the staff gave me lots of grace and I learned quickly that if I was going to improve anything, I was going to need lots of help. My mentor John Maxwell says it best

33

with his law of connection. The law states a leader touches a heart before they ask for a hand. That is so true and I cannot express enough how important it is for a leader to reach out and make a sincere effort to connect with team members. If they do connect, the success they will achieve together will be so much sweeter than a leader using their position to bully and intimidate team members into completing projects or some other top down initiative.

So what's the secret to building relationships? Well, the best advice I can give to a leader is to sincerely want to get to know the staff they supervise and serve. Don't fake it. If you fake it, staff will see right through you.

The next step is to put a plan in place on how you will routinely visit, connect, and speak with staff. The bigger the organization, the more challenging it will be, but in the long run it will be worth it. Taking notes after conversations to remember names and topics is also a great idea.

In one of my districts, after coming across a staff picture from the previous year, I memorized each team member's name and learned a little about each of them. After they came into meet me, I sent them a personal letter inviting them to discuss their ideas for the upcoming year. They were shocked to find I already knew their kids' names and a little about each of them. It paid dividends in the community and with other staff who knew that I had taken the time to get to know them.

Another strategy that I've have used with some success is doing a quick personality test on team members. Doing these kinds of test show a couple things. First, if it's a good test, it shows how people are wired and think. Second, it shows how important each team member is to the whole business. After these tests, I would group team members together who were in the same category and we would discuss strengths and challenges of each. Human beings have natural strengths and weaknesses and great teams utilize each team member's strengths to complete the company's mission and vision.

Can you lose a connection with staff? Yes, you can. If you stop making an effort to connect, you will eventually lose what you worked so hard to achieve. It's like any relationship. You get what you put into it. A good example would be comparing a relationship to a plant. If you water a plant for a while it will grow and flourish, but if you forget to and over time neglect it, it will eventually die, or at a minimum, its growth will be stunted.

Some questions to consider...

- What actions have you taken to build healthy relationships with your staff?

- Which staff are most like you? You will connect naturally with these people.

- Which staff are least like you? These people you will not gravitate towards naturally.

- What is the best way to connect with staff who are not like you?

Tony Robbins leading a personal development training.

INSIGHT # 6
Development

> "Leadership ability determines a person's level of effectiveness."
>
> —John Maxwell

Too OFTEN, WHEN leaders hire new team members, we automatically assume their talent is an 8 or higher on a scale from 1 to 10. The reality is they probably are an 8 in their areas of strength, but much lower in other areas they will need to perform in as well.

One of the biggest mistakes leaders make is plopping these new and existing team members on the workplace game board without having a plan on how they are going to raise their skills. To use a gaming analogy, we need to continue "leveling up" our team members' skills so their upgraded skills can amplify other team members' skills and the overall business. When a business makes this a priority, employee satisfaction goes up and absenteeism and turnover goes down.

I know what you may be thinking. If you improve team members' skills to be better than when you hired them, they will leave and go to work for another company. Yes, you may be right. They may leave your business. But what if they stay? What if they stay because they know you value them and want to invest in them? The bottom line is good things will happen for your business when you invest in your team.

If you don't invest in your team members, they will stay at the level you hired them and that would be sad for them as human beings not having the opportunity to grow. Making it a goal and priority to develop and grow your team members' skill sets is what advanced, forward thinking businesses and leaders do.

Some questions to consider...

- How are you currently upgrading the skills of your team members?

- What trainings have you provided?

- Which team members need training the most?

- What kinds of trainings do you need to provide the most?

Steve Jobs introducing the first iPhone.

INSIGHT # 7
Vision Casting

> Where there is no vision, the people perish: but he that keepeth the law, happy is he.
>
> —Proverbs 29:18

I F YOU WERE to create a list of the most successful leaders, entrepreneurs, or athletes in the world, they would have one thing in common: They believe they can achieve anything. Matter of fact, they envision themselves being successful in whatever challenge they're facing. This vision is so crystal clear that they can see each step in their path to victory.

One of the most important things a leader has to do is cast their vision. They need to share it with their team and stakeholders so that everyone knows the direction the business is heading. And not just once, but they need to recast this vision frequently so that team members don't forget where they're heading. A leader can do this a lot of different ways, but face to face conversations are the most effective. Monthly newsletters, email communications and other forms of traditional communication to share the vision works to a degree, but there is no substitute for good old fashion talking the talk and walking the walk. Staff have to be able to see you doing the work with them side by side to burn into their mind how important the work is that will get them to the vision. Remember, a leader's vision is not where they currently are right now. A vision is the story a leader tells of where they want the organization or business to be in the future. And as Johnny Unitas used to say, "Talk is cheap, let go play the game!" Johnny wasn't one for a lot of talk in the locker room. He believed in action. And like most leaders, putting an action plan into place to ensure the vision becomes a reality is paramount, or the work never gets done to allow the vision to take place.

The story a leader tells about where they're going and how they're going to get there is critical to allow team members to envision the journey. One of my most successful vision castings came after attending a training in Spokane, Washington. The training was about a leader's journey/story arc and I used it to illustrate our organization's journey. For example, we all know during any given year a business, school, organization or person, will encounter challenges. These challenges, if you plot them on a typical Hollywood story arc, starts with everything being hunky dory (ok), and then suddenly, the challenge, or in a Hollywood movie, the killer meteor, is spotted.

In this story arc, the leader and their team will overcome this and other challenges by finding the magic elixir (solution) to the problem. In real life, like the movies, the solution to the challenge often arrives in the form of a new character arriving who knows the secret or has a special skill or ability to solve the problem.

As I shared my vision with the 200+ staff, I overlaid this story arc casting a vision. I shared where we currently were and where we were going, and emphasized that I had faith in our team and that I knew the right characters would show up and help us in our journey to become the school district we all wanted to become. This vision casting was well received by staff, not only because they understood and were very familiar with the Hollywood story arc, but I spoke from my heart with passion, showing that I truly believed we would find a way to achieve our goals.

Some questions to consider...

- What is your vision for your business? Organization? School? District? Remember, vision is not where it currently is, but rather where you want it to be in the future.

- How have you cast your vision as a leader? Family leader?

- How does your team show that they know your vision?

- What is the killer meteor that your facing right now?

General Colin Powell sharing about weapons of mass destruction.

INSIGHT # 8
Stress Management

> When I look back on all these worries, I remember the story of the old man who said on his deathbed that he had had a lot of trouble in his life, most of which had never happened."
>
> —Winston Churchill

W HETHER WE LIKE it or not, stress and leadership tend to go hand in hand and impact many things within an organization. Matter of fact, research shows employees of stressed leaders are six times less likely to be engaged at work. I suppose there are a few leaders out there who have the DNA to be able to shut it off like a light switch, but the majority of us carry it with us home and back to work again day after day. Unfortunately, if you don't have a plan in place for how you will manage the stress of making leadership decisions, it may over time cost you your health, relationships, marriage and quality time with your kids, like it did me. So, what's the secret to managing your stress? Well, it comes down to managing these three things: MIND, BODY, and SPIRIT.

First, the MIND of a leader has to be sharp and focused. This focus allows you as a leader to make well thought out common sense decisions that are at times very complex. These decisions and the stress that comes with them can cause leaders to go into an unhealthy thinking pattern (LOOP), or what Tony Robbins calls a CRAZY EIGHT. The loop is exactly that, your mind goes into a loop and gets stuck thinking about whatever issue(s) you're facing. Leaders who go into this loop too often get labeled as "not able to make timely decisions," as I mentioned in insight # 4, because they over analyze and are seen by staff getting stuck in this loop. Whether you're a formal leader or not, we have all been there when our mind runs situations over and over until our stress level rises.

The CRAZY EIGHT is a more complex loop. But, as your thinking loops on one side of the loop, you get mad, and then you loop and replay how you're going to handle, or should have handled, the situation in your head, like the movie *50 First Dates*. Think about it, have you laid in bed and gotten mad and replayed a past or upcoming event or conversation in your head? If you have, you were probably in one of these two kinds of loops.

So, what's the secret to maintaining a healthy mind and staying away from these loops? Well, you need to do the following:

You need to actually recognize when you're in an unhealthy loop. Sometimes, leaders and people get in the habit of going into these unhealthy loops and come in and out of them for minutes, hours, days or weeks, etc.

You need to shift your focus! Or, in other words, simply intentionally change what you're thinking about.

Consciously do the following:

1. Think about something that you're grateful for.

2. Think about a time or place when you were the happiest.

3. Go for a walk or do something that you enjoy to force yourself out of the environment where your thinking got stuck.

4. Working out releases dopamine and endorphins.

5. Get a massage, it releases serotonin.

6. Cuddle with your partner, it releases Oxytocin.

7. Call your executive coach. Your coach can help you change your unhealthy thinking habits.

Remember, your brain is made up of chemicals and your thoughts increase and decrease levels of both good chemicals D.E.O.S (dopamine, endorphins, oxytocin, serotonin) and bad chemicals like cortisol and adrenaline in your brain. If you're stuck in a negative thought pattern, your brain is increasing its cortisol levels, which is a STRESS hormone in your brain. Elevated cortisol levels can cause insomnia, weight gain, high blood pressure, and the unhealthy list goes on and on.

Secondly, your BODY is directly linked to your mind's health. For example, if the way you handle stress is eating or doing some other unhealthy activity, the symptoms will manifest themselves in your body. It's all connected.

Years ago when I went through my divorce, I went to the doctor and asked for help with my stress at work and with how I was feeling after my divorce. My doctor prescribed me some pill and, of course, there were a number of side effects...weight gain and sleeplessness being two off the top of my head.

The point I'm making is your mind is directly related to your body's performance. If you don't take care of your mind, your body will have problems, and vice versa if you don't take care of your body, your mind will have problems. So, how do you take care of your body?

HERE'S SOME QUICK TIPS THAT YOU ALREADY KNOW:

1. Eat healthy. You are what you eat! If you eat ding dongs you will become a ding dong.

2. At a minimum, complete short workouts each day, e.g., 10 min walks, pushups, sit-ups, yoga poses, etc. Keep it simple!

3. Be aware that if you take medications, you will have side effects whether you like it or not. Ask your doctor what the side effects will be.

Finally, SPIRIT, which is actually defined as the nonphysical part of a person that is the seat of emotions and character; the soul. As a leader, your character and soul must be healthy. If you are involved with activities that hurt your character/soul, you will not be able to lead at the level you must. And, of course, your SPIRIT is directly linked to both your MIND and BODY!

Leadership guru and my mentor John Maxwell sums it up with his law of modeling and law of addition. The law of modeling states that leaders will naturally follow leaders that are stronger than themselves. If you're a leader whose character and SPIRIT is questionable, you won't have too many people wanting to follow you. The law of addition states that leaders add value by serving others. Maxwell says that we add value to others when we truly value them and intentionally make ourselves valuable to them. One way he says we can do this is to sincerely get to know the people we are leading and find out their goals, dreams and hopes, and then figuring out what you can do to help them.

Here's some quick tips to keep your SPIRIT healthy:

1. If you're Christian, go to church. If you a Buddhist, go to the temple. If you're Muslim, go to the mosque. If you're one of the naturalists, go out into nature. And remember, Love and Peace is the only way.

2. Don't participate in activities that will damage your character/spirit.

3. Prayer and meditation are known to release dopamine and endorphins and other healthy brain chemicals. As a leader, you need all the help you can get!

Having a healthy Mind, Body, and Spirit is the key to maintaining manageable stress levels. Stress is a burden of leadership and if you want to be a good leader, making it priority to manage your stress is important.

Ronald Reagan, 40th President of the United States

INSIGHT # 9
Hiring: Talent vs. Loyalty

> Loyalty means giving me your honest opinion, whether you think I'll like it or not. Disagreement at this stage stimulates me. But once a decision has been made, the debate ends. From that point on, loyalty means executing the decision as if it were your own.
>
> —General Colin Powell

TALENT VERSUS LOYALTY is a topic that leaders have grappled with for hundreds of years. I know that I've grappled with the question myself. Should a leader hire someone who is extremely talented, but may have loyalty/character issues? Or should they hire someone who is loyal, but not as talented?

Early in my career, I hired the later, and now in retrospect, I believe some of those hiring decisions may have been mistakes.

Why? Well, there is much more to a person than talent. I was trained, and we all have heard, you're supposed to hire people who are smarter than ourselves. I always tried to do this by hiring the person (male or female) who brought talent and often the skills that I believed my organization needed or lacked. These talented people would show up, and like we expected, brought the skills needed. However, unfortunately they also brought with them some other behaviors that I mentioned in insight #4. For example, often these talented people brought with them egos so big that they could barely fit their heads through the door. Some also brought communication issues that created more drama than their talent was worth. Some also brought ethical issues that I would address and then we would have to start the costly hiring process all over again.

Now, I believe that hiring people who have loyalty and character, and can be trained and developed, is what leaders should consider, in most cases. Hire people who are loyal, believe in your vision, and bring other innate skills, like EQ (emotional intelligence) and PQ (passion quotient). Now, don't get me wrong; these people have to have some level of talent, they cannot be someone who can't do the job. They must have the ability to be coached and learn whatever skills may be necessary for the position.

I've found that people who have a high EQ not only have the ability to relate with others, but also the ability to help your vision become a reality through their relational skills. The same applies for people who have a high PQ (passion quotient). Their passion for the work and for your vision may amplify your business and ultimately your success as a leader. Now remember, people with PQ and EQ could ultimately turn on you when the chips are down and that first crisis hits. But, if you have done a good job of connecting with them and nurturing a healthy relationship, they will hold the line and help you get through the storms that come and go as a leader. As a leader, you will find out quickly who has your back and who doesn't when the crisis hits. The ones who are loyal will be there right beside you, and the ones that aren't, won't be.

A good example of this loyalty question is Russell Wilson of the Seattle Seahawks. He was selected in the 3rd round and was the 75th pick overall of the 2012 NFL draft. Many believed Wilson was undersized at 5'10" and had average arm strength for an NFL quarterback. Wilson, though, had intangibles that many leaders look for when hiring. He had PQ (passion quotient) off the charts and also was known for his loyalty to his team, leadership and work ethic.

Ultimately, as the leader, you will have the final say on hiring. There may be a committee that makes a recommendation, but ultimately, you will need to wrestle with the decision of hiring for talent versus loyalty. You might consider adding the following questions, or some version of them that fits, during an interview:

1. How do you find working for your current employer?

    a. Does the candidate criticize?

2. Tell us about a stressful situation you have gone through at work and how you handled it.

    b. Does the candidate mention working as a team?

3. What is the ideal workplace?

    c. Do they mention teamwork, etc.?

4. What's something you can add to this organization?

    d. Do they mention loyalty or teamwork?

5. Tell me about a situation where you had to go above and beyond to get the job done.

Some questions to consider...

- How does your business currently screen for loyalty?

- What is most important to your business loyalty or talent?

- Who would you consider loyal in business?

- How do you define loyalty in your organization?

Franklin D. Roosevelt, 32nd President of the United States

INSIGHT # 10

Think Big

"Start small, think big. Don't worry about too many things at once. Take a handful of simple things to begin with, and then progress to more complex ones. Think about not just tomorrow, but the future. Put a ding in the universe."

—Steve Jobs

O NE OF THE best pieces of advice I ever received was from my coach and friend Dan Farrell. I met Dan as I took the reins in the Brewster School District in 2007. The year prior, Dan had been the district's interim super-intendent. He had a great way about him as a leader (e.g. gave out Musketeers candy bars to emphasize teamwork) and seemed to have an awareness of his role as a mentor. Unfortunately, as I took the job, I was so busy getting my feet on the ground that I didn't spend the time with him I should have. Dan passed away years ago now, but his coaching has always served me well.

Actually, some of the greatest leaders were known for "thinking big" and making great things happen during their career. One example would be Thailand's late King Bhumibol Adulyadej, who was known for his many social and economic development projects throughout his country. If you ever visit Thailand, you will see his vision as a leader still benefits the people of that beautiful country.

Franklin Delano Roosevelt was also known for "thinking big" with his New Deal programs of the 1930's. He started the programs to help the United States recover from the Great Depression. Hoover Dam, which is a 45-minute drive from Las Vegas, is a result of his thinking big.

Bill Gates, Steve Jobs, Jeff Bezos, and Elon Musk are all known for "thinking big" and being game changers for their respective companies. Their ability to "think big" is also a result of having a talented team around them, as well. Some of my "biggest ideas" and most significant leadership moves came as a result of being inspired by the team of people I had around me.

Some questions to consider...

- What "big ideas" do you have for your business in the next year? In the next five years?

- Who do you have or need on your team to inspire you?

- Who on your team inspires you?

- Who on your team is the "Debbie Downer" or limits the team's potential?

Follow effective action with quiet reflection. From the quiet reflection will come even more effective action.

—Peter F. Drucker

Summary

I HOPE THESE TEN insights and the reflective questions in each
chapter will serve not only new and up and coming leaders, but
also as a quick reminder to more veteran leaders. Too often, all
of us get caught up in day-to-day work or crisis and we forget to
reflect on what we have learned over a period of time. Reflection
is said to turn experience into insight. John Maxwell's Law of
Reflection states that to grow, we must intentionally learn from
past experiences, both failures and successes. When you have an
experience that challenges you as a leader and as a human being,
sit down, take out your journal and write a reflection on things
you feel went well and things that you need to do better the next
time around.

In the back of this book, I've included some tools I personally
use that will help you in your journey as a leader and parent. If
you would like a digital copy please email me at gladiatorcoach@
icloud.com

I have included the following:

- A decision-making protocol that will help you make decisions when you have several options to consider. It will also help you look at the consequences that come with each option.

- A stress management protocol that will help you as leader (or anyone, for that matter) pinpoint your stress and put an action plan in place to begin dealing with it in a healthy way.

- I've also included a simple tool that will help you develop a 5-year plan for your life, business, and your family.

Here are the ten insights contained in this book for your review:

1. **Influence:** Every leader has people around them who are trying to influence them in some way. Be careful who is in your inner circle, because those closest to you (your team) will reduce or expand your potential as a leader.

   a. Who is your Wormtongue?

   b. Who is your Gandalf?

2. **Documentation:** Leaders are obligated to interact and connect with different kinds of people on a daily basis. Because of this, they should make it a habit to document these interactions, creating a trail of evidence. Some ways to accomplish this:

   a. Journaling

   b. Quick summary emails to themselves

c. Have a witness present during interactions.

3. **Bad Apples:** Leaders have to be aware of these three different types of bad apples because research has shown that they can reduce team performance by up to 30%. Remember, bad apples can increase turnover and decrease employee engagement just to name a few!

   a. Who are your bad apples?

   b. How are they currently affecting your business?

4. **Hazardous Leadership Behaviors:** World leaders, famous actors, and even you and I can show these behaviors if we don't monitor our intentions and hearts closely.

   a. Which of these behaviors have you seen in yourself?

   b. Which of these behaviors have you seen in others?

5. **Relationships:** John Maxwell says it best with his law of connection. The law states a leader touches a heart before they ask for a hand. Building strong, healthy relationships with team members has to be a top priority to truly see success as a leader.

   a. Who do you need to build a relationship with?

   b. How does building a relationship with staff help you further down the road?

6. **Development:** Developing your team members beyond the level they were hired should be a top priority for all leaders. If you hire someone who is a six in talent, on a one to ten scale, they will not grow beyond that level

unless you make growth and development an institutional priority.

    a. How are you currently developing your staff?

    b. In what areas do you need to focus future development?

7. **Vision Casting:** Leaders have to make it a priority to find ways to cast their visions for their organization/business. If you do this well, stakeholders will know that the best is yet to come.

    a. What is your vision for your organization?

    b. How have you casted this vision?

8. **Stress Management:** Stress and Leadership go hand in hand. As a leader, you have an obligation to both your staff and your family to find ways to manage your stress.

    a. On a scale from one to ten, what is your current stress level?

    b. How do you currently manage your stress?

9. **Talent versus Loyalty (Character):** This is a hiring question that many leaders struggle with because they're trained to hire people who are smarter than they are. I believe leaders should hire, in most cases, for loyalty (character) because these team members will stand with you when the storms of leadership come.

    a. What is most important to you, talent or loyalty?

    b. How does hiring for character/loyalty help your business in the future?

10. **Think Big**: Great leaders have vision and make *thinking big* a priority for their team and organization. Steve Jobs and Elon Musk are just a few well-known leaders who have carved out their historical legacy by thinking big.

   a. What *big ideas* do you have for the upcoming year?

   b. How will big ideas affect the future of your business?

Decision Making Protocol

Date:

Name:

What is your overarching goal that directly relates to the decision that you have to make?

Step 1: What decision do you need to make?

Step 2: What are the options?

Option 1:

Option 2:

Option 3:

Step 3: What are the consequences for each option?

Consequences for Option 1:

Consequences for Option 2:

Consequences for Option 3:

Step 4: What is the most logical option that helps you achieve your overarching goal?

6 months later...

Step 5: What were the actual consequences of your decision?

Stress Management Protocol

Date:

Name:

1. What is your current stress level on a scale of 1 to 10?

2. Who/What is currently causing you stress?

3. What activities are you currently doing to manage your stress?

4. What actions are you taking to correct the things causing you stress?

5. How often does your thinking go into a loop? Once a week? Once a day?

6. When you're under stress, what symptoms manifest themselves? Irritability? Depression?

7. How many times and how long do you estimate you go into a loop or unhealthy thinking patterns each day? Week?

8. What is the thought or activity that takes you out of an unhealthy thought pattern?

9. Who is someone who can help you create healthy thought patterns?

10. What are your next action steps to manage your stress?

    Action 1:

       a. Start Date:

    Action 2:

       b. Start Date:

    Action 3:

       c. Start Date:

Five-year plan

Date:

Name:

Goal:

Actions (Areas of study, training, specific actions, etc.)

Year 1:

Year 2:

Year 3:

Year 4:

Year 5:

Notes

Notes

Notes

Ideas!

Ideas!

Ideas!

Ideas!

Made in the USA
San Bernardino, CA
01 February 2018